DISCLAIMER: This is an UN original book.

MW00977966

It designed to record all the key points of the original book.

It helps you get an overview before or after reading the original book.

If you haven't owned the original book, you can buy it here:

https://www.amazon.com/dp/ B07D23CFGR

This book is not authorized, approved, licensed, or endorsed by the subject book's author or publisher. **Keynotes** is not associated with the original author in any way.

Table of Contents

Introduction

This book revolves around the idea that the quality of our habits decides the quality of our lives. Too many of us are living without a sense of discipline or awareness of our habits. We sometimes believe that we cannot get better or improve our lives because we just do not have the ability to change anything. This book will teach us how to change our habits to live a better and more successful life.

Background

The author of this book, James Clear, experienced a life-altering injury on the last day of his sophomore year of high school. As Clear's classmate took a swing, his baseball bat slipped from his hands, flew towards Clear and hit him between the eyes in full force. Clear was rushed to the hospital. It broke Clear's nose into a U-shape. His brain's soft tissue crashed into his skull's interior surface. He later had a seizure and could not remember some basic things properly. The incident left him with several skull fractures and a distorted eye. His eyeball dangled out of its socket. A helicopter flew Clear and his mother to a bigger hospital in Cincinnati and his father joined them later after leaving his siblings with relatives. His parents had become familiar with this hospital ten years before when Clear's sister had been diagnosed with leukemia at the age of three. James was five and his brother just six months old at the time. His sister recovered after two and a half years of chemotherapy treatments and other complicated procedures. Clear had to be put into a coma briefly but was removed from it later.

Clear's recovery was slow and steady. He had double vision for weeks following the incident. His eyeball went back to its original place after more than a month. He was able to drive a car after eight months. James had played baseball since he was a child. It was in his blood. However, he could not return to the baseball field before a year had passed. He was cut from the varsity baseball team which disappointed him greatly. After one more year, he was able to join the varsity team as a senior but only managed to play eleven innings in high school. However, even though he could not do much during his high school baseball career, he believed that he could do better. When he started college at Denison University two years after his injury, it changed everything.

The Knowledge about Habits

Clear was happy to join the baseball team at Denison University. He started developing good habits. Unlike other students who stayed up late and played video games, he began going to bed early. He also kept his dorm room tidy and clean. These small steps helped him enjoy a sense of control over his life. His confidence began to return and translated into good grades. He earned straight A's during his first year in college.

Habits are behaviors or routines that unfold consistently and even automatically at times too. As his college journey progressed, he gathered tiny but regular habits that helped him reach outcomes that seemed impossible earlier.

By his junior year, Clear had been voted team captain and at the season's finish, he was selected for the all-conference team. His habits of sleep, study, and strength-training really began leading to significant results during his senior year. Six years after his injury, he was chosen as the top male athlete at Denison University and named to the ESPN Academic All-America Team. He was also awarded the University's top honor, the President's Medal. He never played professionally but reached his potential with the help of his habits.

Journey toward this Book

In November 2012, Clear started publishing articles at jamesclear.com. These articles were based on Clear's years of experiments with habits. Within a few months, he had gained his first 1000 email subscribers. By the time 2013 concluded, the number of Clear's subscribers had gone beyond 30,000 people. In 2014, Clear's email list had increased to more than one hundred thousand subscribers.

In 2015, the author gained 200,000 email subscribers and signed a book deal with Penguin Random House for this book. With his audience multiplying, his business prospects also grew. He was repeatedly asked by prominent firms to speak about habit creation, behavior alteration, and continual improvement. He was asked to deliver important speeches at conferences in Europe and the United States.

In 2016, his articles started getting published in publications such as Forbes, Time, and Entrepreneur. NBA, NFL, and MLB coaches started reading Clear's articles and sharing them with their teams. Clear established the Habits Academy, which acquired the status of being the main training arena for people and companies that wanted to adopt improved habits in both life and work. Developing start-ups and Fortune 500 firms also started registering their leaders and training their employees. More than 10,000 leaders, coaches, managers, and educators have graduated from the Habits Academy. When James was finalizing this book in 2018, his website was receiving millions of monthly visitors and almost 500,000 email newsletter weekly subscribers.

The Book

The author had to live the ideas/small habits in the book to come back from his injury, perform better, be a writer, establish a business, and become a responsible person. The writer will share a detailed plan to build better habits for our entire lives.

The Very Basics: Why Small Changes Lead to Huge Differences

Chapter 1: Atomic Habits can Lead to Stunning Results

The author cites the example of how the destiny of British Cycling completely transformed in 2003 after hiring Dave Brailsford. He made the most of changing small habits and things regarding the riders, their surroundings, and equipment. The rest is history.

Why Small Habits Can Change Everything

Massive success does not always require huge changes. Only 1% of change can change things in the long run. When we introduce 1% changes, we might not be able to notice things initially but they make a huge difference. If we improve 1% daily for a year, we will be 37 times better by the end of it. If we get 1% worse daily for a year, we will be near zero by its end.

Our habits multiply in their impact with their repetition. They might not seem to make a huge difference in a single day but their impact over the months and years is gigantic. You will realize the impact of good or bad habits after two, five, or ten years.

It is hard for us to realize the significance of good habits since they do not seem to matter in the current moment. If we save a small amount of money today, we won't realize its importance immediately since it will not make us millionaires right now. If we study a language we don't know for an hour today, we still will not have learned it. We will not lose any weight despite going to the gym consecutively for a number of days.

Bad habits can also be disguised this way. If we eat unhealthy food today, it does not seem to make a huge difference. If we choose to work late and ignore our family today, it won't seem to matter much. However, these 1% habits can lead to disastrous results later. Our habits accumulate and lead to the kind of outcomes that define the course of our lives. Success is the outcome of our habits instead of overnight transformation. When 1% good or 1% bad habits accumulate over time, they can play a huge role in defining our destiny. Don't be too occupied with whether you are currently successful or not. What matters is whether you have the right habits and if they are driving you toward success or not.

Our outcomes make a statement about our habits. Our net worth exposes our financial habits. Our weight shows our eating habits. Our knowledge stems from our learning habits. Our clutter highlights our cleaning habits.

Good habits turn time into our friend. Bad habits turn it into our enemy. Habits can lead to both positive and negative compounding. Several former actions give rise to breakthrough moments. These actions create the potential needed to trigger substantial change. Habits do not seem to matter at all until we surpass a crucial threshold and open the doors to something new. When we start something and our progress does not show initially, we get disappointed. We need to understand that during substantial compounding, the most effective results experience a delay.

This is why developing lasting habits is so difficult. People start something but when they do not see results right away, they give up. When we cross the threshold after working hard steadily, it seems like overnight success to people. However, we have been working hard to achieve it for a long time. The efforts we put in a long time ago were what made all this success possible. This is why constant hard work matters.

Patience makes mastery possible. When something finally happens as a result of an action, it is not the action that makes it possible. It was all the hard work that preceded that particular action. A small decision comes before a habit and paves the way for it.

Systems are More Important than Goals

We run after goals but the best way to accomplish something is to focus on the systems we use instead of goals. Goals pertain to the outcomes we wish to accomplish. Systems refer to the processes that make those outcomes possible. For example, an entrepreneur's goal might be to establish a million-dollar business. Their system is the way they test product ideas, hire workers, and conduct marketing campaigns. A coach's goal might be to win a championship. Their system is the manner in which they recruit players, supervise their assistant coaches, and carry out practice.

You Can Succeed by Improving your Systems and Ignoring Your Goals

The most important point in this context is that you can succeed by focusing on and improving your systems and completely ignoring your goals. For example, our goal in any sport is to achieve the highest score. But if we kept looking at the scoreboard during the entire game, it would be crazy. We can only win by improving daily. Goals are not entirely worthless. They help define a direction but the systems are what help us make progress.

Some Problems that Occur When We Focus More on Goals than Systems

Problem 1: Winners and Losers Share Identical Goals

Goals do not make people win the Olympics or any other championship. Everyone who is playing has the same goal, including winners and losers. It's not the goal that made someone the winner. It was implementation of a system of continual betterment that helped them achieve a better outcome.

Problem 2: Accomplishing a Goal is Just Instantaneous Change

If our room is always messy and we have a motivational episode in which we clean it up but do not change our hoarding habits, it will be cluttered again. This only leads to momentary change. We need to treat the cause rather than the symptoms for lasting change. In this case, accomplishing a goal only changed our life in the moment. We need to change our systems instead of our results. If we rectify our inputs, it will automatically correct our outputs.

Problem 3: Goals Limit Our Joy

When we equate happiness with goals, we postpone happiness until we accomplish the next goal. This stops us from being happy in the moment. It also causes us to limit ourselves. If we accomplish our goals, we believe we are successful. If we do not accomplish our goals, we consider ourselves failures. When you focus more on your system, it will make you happy when it is running well. A system has so many dimensions that it can be successful in several ways, even if it deviates from what you expected.

Problem 4: Goals and Long-Term Progress Cancel Each Other

If a goal is the only thing that motivates us, we will stop working after we achieve it. With this mindset, a runner will stop training after a race. A goal-oriented person will lose all motivation to work after accomplishing a goal. Proper long-term thinking operates without goals. Determination to the process decides our progress.

A System Consisting of Atomic Habits

If we fail to change our habits despite trying, our system is wrong. We might have the incorrect system for change. You are what your systems are. This book's themes include focusing on all aspects of the system instead of on one goal. An atomic habit is a very small change or a 1% improvement. Atomic habits do not just mean any habits. They are part of an overall system. Atomic habits serve as the building blocks to wonderful results. Habits further serve as our life's atoms. Every single habit acts as a basic unit that plays a role in our improvement. These small routines might seem unimportant initially but they strengthen alongside one another and contribute to more substantial success. They become quite large in their impact. Therefore, atomic habits refer to a consistent routine that is tiny, easy to perform, and the root of a lot of power. It is a constituent of a system of compound growth.

Core Lessons from the Chapter:

- Get 1% better every day because these small improvements will accumulate and make a huge difference in your life.

- Focus on improving your systems instead of concentrating on your goals.

Chapter 2: Our Habits Define Our Identity (and vice versa)

We find it extremely difficult to keep our good habits going after the initial burst of motivation. On the other hand, once a habit becomes established, it does not leave us, especially the bad ones. Even though we want to change, unhealthy habits such as smoking, eating junk food, procrastinating, or watching television all the time seem impossible to get rid of.

We find it difficult to change our habits for two reasons. We focus on changing the wrong thing. We try to transform our habits in the wrong manner.

Behavior Change: Three Layers

Change happens at three levels or layers. The first layer is changing our outcomes. This means changing our results. The second layer is changing our process. This means changing our systems and habits. The third layer pertains to the act of changing our identity. It means changing our beliefs, views, self–image, and our judgment of ourselves and others. Outcomes pertain to what we receive. Processes pertain to what we do. Identity pertains to what we believe. Every single level matters in the context of 1% improvement. However, we have to be careful about the direction of change.

Most of us try to start changing our habits by altering what we wish to accomplish, which paves the way for outcome-based habits. We need identity-based habits. This means we should start by concentrating on who we want to be.

Outcome-Based vs. Identity-Based Habits

Consider two people who say no to a cigarette. The first one says something like, "No thanks. I'm trying to quit." This person is focusing on the outcome but still considers himself to be a smoker. Another person trying to quit answers the offer by saying, "No thanks. I'm not a smoker." This person is focusing on an identity change. Those who follow an outcome-based approach set goals and then try to decide what actions they need to take to accomplish those goals minus thinking about the beliefs that direct their actions. They do not alter the way they consider themselves.

Every system of actions works based on a system of beliefs. Beliefs and assumptions play a role in the system. An identity determines our habits. When we take pride in a component of our identity, we will have the desired motivation to sustain the habits linked with it. We might begin a habit because of motivation but we will only stick to it if it finds a place in our identity.

For example, the goal should be to become a reader, instead of reading a book. The goal should be to become a runner, instead of running a marathon. The goal should be to become a musician, instead of learning an instrument. When something becomes part of our identity, we can adhere to it and it will work against us if it prevents us from changing. For example, we might label ourselves as someone who is bad with directions, not a morning person, always late, etc. When we keep telling ourselves these kinds of stories over several years, we begin to accept them as fact. It becomes extremely difficult to change an action or thought that has a strong link to our identity. If we want to become our best version, we will need to edit our beliefs continually and update and extend our identity.

Transforming your Identity: A Two-Step Process

Our identity stems from our habits. We do not have preset beliefs. Each belief is learned and conditioned. When we reinforce a behavior, we reinforce the identity linked with that behavior.

To change who we are, we need to change what we do. For example, every time we write a page, we are a writer. Each time we begin a workout, we are an athlete. When we keep doing something, we start believing that we can achieve these things. It keeps adding up and strengthening our identity in that direction. It works this way for bad habits too.

The Two-Step Process

1. Determine the kind of person you wish to become.

2. Prove it to yourself with the help of small wins.

The first step works both individually and collectively. What are your values and principles? Who do you want to be? Since most of us know the results we want to achieve, we can begin there and work out who we want to be to achieve those results. We need to ask ourselves, who is the kind of person who can achieve these results? Who is the kind of person that can successfully handle a start-up? Who is the kind of person that can learn a new language? Who is the kind of person that can write a book?

The answer to the last question is someone dependable and consistent. This will shift our focus from writing a book (outcome-based) to becoming the kind of person who is dependable and consistent (identity-based). This process can give birth to beliefs such as 'I am the type of teacher who supports her students' or 'I am the type of manager who stands up for their workers.'

The author's friend lost 100 pounds by asking herself the question, "What would a healthy person do?" In every situation, she chose what a healthy person chose and successfully lost more than 100 pounds. Identity-based habits bring us into feedback loops. Our habits determine our identity and our identity determines our habits. It's a bidirectional process. Habit creation works in the form of a feedback loop. It is crucial for our identity, principles, and values to direct the loop instead of our results.

We should always focus on becoming a certain kind of person instead of getting a specific outcome.

Why Habits Matter

The most significant question is who is it that we wish to become? Our identity is not unchangeable. We have the ability to transform our beliefs about ourselves. We always have a choice. We can select the identity we want to reinforce today with the habits that we select today. Habits are about becoming someone rather than having something. Our habits help us form beliefs about ourselves. We become our habits.

Core Lessons from the Chapter:

- Focus on who you want to be to change your habits.

- Update your beliefs and extend your identity continuously for being the best 'you.'

Chapter 3: Forming Better Habits Takes these 4 Steps

The four steps of habit formation can be divided into two phases. These include the problem phase and the solution phase. The problem phase encompasses the cue and the craving. It happens when we recognize that we need to change something. The solution phase includes the response and the reward. It happens when we do something and accomplish the change we desire.

The desire to change something directs every behavioral pattern. At times, the problem might be that we observe a positive thing and want to get it for ourselves. At other times, the problem might be that we are going through pain and want to relieve it. A lot of our real life actions go through these steps.

The Four Laws of Behavior Change

Formation of a Good Habit

- The 1st Law (Cue): Make it apparent/obvious.

- The 2nd Law (Craving): Make it appealing/attractive.

- The 3rd Law (Response): Make it easy.

- The 4th Law (Reward): Make it satisfying.

Breaking a Bad Habit

We can break a bad habit by inverting these laws.

- The 1st Law Inverted (Cue): Make it invisible.

- The 2nd Law Inverted (Craving): Make it unappealing.

- The 3rd Law Inverted (Response): Make it challenging.

- The 4th Law Inverted (Reward): Make it unsatisfying.

These four laws provide the framework to change any behavior. They apply to every single field. We don't need separate strategies for different habits.

When we wish to change our behavior, we can just ask ourselves the following questions:

1. How can I make it clear/apparent/obvious?
2. How can I make it appealing?
3. How can I make it easy?
4. How can I make it satisfying?

The systems in our lives determine our habits. Subsequent chapters will teach us how to use these laws to build a system which will automatically lead to good habits and repel bad ones.

Core Lessons from the Chapter:

- To build good habits, make them obvious, appealing, easy, and satisfying.

- To avoid bad habits, make them invisible, unappealing, challenging, and unsatisfying.

The 1st Law: Make it Clear/Obvious.

Chapter 4: The Man who Didn't Appear to be Right

The cues that ignite our habits become so common over time that they are invisible. The phone in our pocket, the remote control beside the couch, etc. are such cues. Our responses to these cues are programmed to such a degree that it seems like the impulse to act stems from nowhere. Therefore, we need to start the process of behavior change with awareness. However, before building new habits, we need to control the current ones.

The Habits Scorecard

The Japanese railway system is among the best in the world. Every employee uses the process of pointing-and-calling to lessen mistakes. Pointing-and-calling works effectively because it increases the awareness level from a non-conscious habit to a more conscious level. For example, we can use this system before leaving the house to remember that we have everything including our keys, wallet, glasses, phone, etc. by naming it loudly. When a behavior becomes increasingly automatic, we stop thinking about it consciously. When we have done something many times, we start overlooking things. We may think that it will execute like the last time but it won't. Our performance declines because of a lack of self-awareness.

While transforming habits, one of the hardships we experience is sustaining awareness of what action we are taking. We require a point-and-call system in our lives. This provides the foundation for the Habits Scorecard. It is a basic exercise to raise our awareness regarding our behavior. We should create a list of our daily habits.

A sample list is as follows:

Wake up, switch off alarm, go through my phone, make a washroom visit, check my weight, take a shower, brush my teeth, floss my teeth, put on cologne, hang up towel, put on clothes, prepare a cup of coffee/tea.

After completing your list, ask yourself whether it is a good, bad, or neutral habit. Form a '+' sign next to it if it is a good habit, a '-' sign if it is a bad habit, and an '=' sign if it is a neutral habit.

Whether a habit is good or bad depends on a person's situation. For a person trying to lose weight, high-calorie foods will be a minus. For a person trying to gain muscle, such food will be a plus. Scoring habits can be especially difficult since no habits are good or bad. Habits are only effective at solving problems. So classify your habits by their impact on you in the long run.

When you are in the middle of preparing your scorecard, you don't need to change anything. Just observe. Do it without any positive or negative judgment. You can use the pointing-and-calling process as well.

Core Lessons from the Chapter:

- We need to be aware of our habits before changing them.

- We can use the methods of pointing-and-calling and the Habits Scorecard to achieve awareness.

Chapter 5: The Preferred Manner to Begin a New Habit

Implementation intentions help us adhere to our goals. The basic format of an implementation intention is:

When situation X emerges, I will carry out response Y.

When we write down the exact date and time of an action, we are likely to actually do it whether it means quitting smoking, sleeping early, studying, etc. Voter turnout increases when voters are asked to respond to questions about the route they will take, the time they will go, or the bus they will take.

The most significant cues are time and location. In other words, for those who map out a detailed plan for the time and place they will carry out a new habit, there is a higher probability that they will go through with their intended plans. A lot of people try to alter their habits without planning these details, only to fail. A lot of people think they don't have the motivation when they just need clarity. People do not know the time and place to take action and end up wasting time.

After underlining an implementation intention, we do not need to wait for inspiration. When the time for action arrives, we just need to act in accord with our preset plan.

We can use this strategy for our habits in the following way:

I will [BEHAVIOR] at [TIME] in [LOCATION].

Examples:

Studying: I will study French for 30 minutes at 5 pm in my room.

Exercise: I will work out for an hour at 4 pm in the gym.

The Usefulness of Habit Stacking

The Diderot Effect states that when we acquire a new possession, it leads to a chain of consumption which encompasses other purchases. This is evident from the example that when we purchase a dress, we want matching shoes and earrings as well. Several human behaviors also adhere to this spiral. We determine what to do based on what we have just done. Behaviors do not unfold in isolation. Actions become cues that trigger subsequent behaviors.

This is crucial because when it comes to habit formation, we can make the most of behavioral interlinking. For new habit formation, we can recognize an existing habit we repeat every day and then stack our new behavior on top of it. This is known as habit stacking.

Habit stacking is a particular type of implementation intention. In this type, we couple our new habit with an existing one instead of a time and location.

The habit stacking formula is:

After [CURRENT HABIT], I will [NEW HABIT].

Examples:

Meditation: After drinking my cup of tea every morning, I will meditate for two minutes.

Thankfulness: After I seat myself to dinner, I will share one thing I am grateful for that happened today.

We need to link our required behavior with something we do daily. We can locate the 'trigger' for our habit stack by using the Habit Scorecard. We can also create a new list with two columns. We can compose the first column by writing down what we do daily. This will include getting out of bed, showering, brushing our teeth, and so on until we get into bed. In the second column, we will write things that happen daily. Examples include the sun rising, a text message coming, and the sun setting. Be as specific as possible in your habit stacks since ambiguity does not work.

Core Lessons from the Chapter:

Implementation intention formula:

I will [BEHAVIOR] at [TIME] in [LOCATION].

Habit stacking formula:

After [CURRENT HABIT], I will [NEW HABIT].

Chapter 6: Environment is More Important than Motivation

Our habits change based on where we are (the room we are in) and the cues we notice. The invisible factor that leaves an effect on our behavior is the environment. Specific environmental factors cause some specific behaviors to repeat regardless of peoples' unique personalities. Change is external in this context. Our surroundings transform us. Context plays a huge role in our habits.

We think we are in control but a lot of times, the most apparent options direct our choices. Sensory cues are extremely significant and the most important of these is vision.

Designing Our Environment for Success

Forming clear visual cues can direct our attention towards a required habit. Each habit is triggered by a cue.

How to Use Visual Cues

If you don't want to miss your medication, place the bottle next to the faucet in the washroom.

If you want to remember to play guitar regularly, put your guitar stand in the center of the living room.

If you want to compose more thank you notes, place your stationery on your desk. If you want to drink more water, fill a few water bottles and place them in visible places around the house.

To adopt a habit, add a cue visibly to the environment. Small context changes can give rise to substantial behavior changes over time. Each habit results from a cue. If the cue is obvious, we are more likely to observe it. Therefore, we need to make cues apparent in our environment.

With the passage of time, our habits start getting linked with the overall context encompassing the behavior instead of just one trigger. The context acquires the status of the cue. This is why it is easier to form new habits in a new environment since we do not have to battle old cues in that case.

Core Lessons from the Chapter:

Make the cues of good habits apparent in your setting. This will help make the context the cue.

Chapter 7: How to Approach Self-Control

Drug addicts are able to get rid of their addiction in a rehabilitation center because of the new environment. When most of them return home, they become addicted again because of old cues such as the people and places they used to associate with. Research indicates that those who seem to have more self-control or discipline are not different from those without self-control. They actually avoid spending time in tempting circumstances.

In other words, those who have to use their self-control the least have the best self-control.

Get Rid of the Cue that Causes a Bad Habit

The most effective way to avoid a bad habit is to lessen exposure to the cue that causes it.

Examples:

If you feel unable to get any work done, keep your phone in another room for a few hours. If you have been feeling inadequate, unfollow the social media accounts that make you feel this way. If you watch television excessively, remove the TV from your bedroom. If you shop too much, stop reading product reviews and looking at sales ads. If you are playing video games excessively, keep the console in a closet when you are not using it. This is the inversion of the 1st Law of Behavior Change. Make it invisible. Since self-control can only work as a short-term strategy, design your environment so that it will stop tempting you.

Core Lessons from the Chapter:

- Make bad habits invisible.

- To get rid of a bad habit, lessen exposure to the cue that causes it.

The 2nd Law: Make it Appealing/Attractive

Chapter 8: Making a Habit Irresistible

Like animals, humans are also susceptible to fall for exaggerated versions of reality. This is why we are prone to consume junk foods. Food is available abundantly but our body still acts like it is scarce like old times. We crave the high salt, sugar, and fat content in junk food. It makes our reward systems crazy.

When an opportunity is extremely attractive, it can play a huge role in habit formation. Habits operate in the form of a dopamine-drive feedback loop. Our motivation to do something increases with an increase in dopamine. We do something when we anticipate a reward, not when we fulfill it. The rise in dopamine is directly proportional to anticipation. We can use temptation bundling to increase the attractiveness of new habits. In temptation bundling, we use something we really want to do along with something we don't want to do since the first will make the second possible.

The formula of habit stacking + temptation bundling:

1. **After [CURRENT HABIT], I will [HABIT I NEED].**

43

2. After [HABIT I NEED], I will [HABIT I WANT].

For example, if you need to express more gratitude and want to read the news, it will unfold the following way:

1. After I drink my morning tea, I will state one thing I am grateful for that happened yesterday (need).

2. After I state the thing I am grateful for, I will go through the news.

This strategy will enable us to look forward to what we *need* to do to proceed to what we *want* to do.

Core Lessons from the Chapter:

The formula of habit stacking + temptation bundling:

1. After [CURRENT HABIT], I will [HABIT I NEED].

2. After [HABIT I NEED], I will [HABIT I WANT].

Chapter 9: How Family and Friends Determine Our Habits

The behaviors that seem most attractive to us are the ones that are a norm of our culture. Human beings operate in herds and wish to fit in. We want to connect with others and seek their approval.

We most commonly replicate the behavior of three groups:

1. Those who are close to us.
2. Those who are many.
3. Those who enjoy power.

1. Imitating those who are close

Proximity leaves a significant effect on our behavior. We are likely to copy the behaviors of those closest to us. According to research, we face more probability of being obese if a friend is obese. Similarly, if one partner in a relationship loses weight, the other partner is likely to lose weight as well.

2. Imitating those who are many

We tend to act like a group. When the number of people in a group increases, so does our level of conformity. When we are uncertain of the way we should act, we seek guidance from the group to direct our behavior. We read Amazon and other reviews to see what others are doing. We wish to replicate the most popular purchasing, food, and travel habits.

The regular behavior of the group surpasses the desired behavior of a person. We experience interior pressure to succumb to the group's norms. We prefer to be wrong along with the group than to be right individually. Change is appealing when changing our habits means synchronizing with the tribe. Change is unappealing when changing our habits means going against the tribe.

3. Imitating those with power

All of us seek status and power. We want to be identified and appreciated. We run after titles and badges. This is why people who are more powerful are more attractive. We are pulled toward behaviors that will help us gain acceptance, respect, praise, and status. This is why we are so interested in the habits of extremely influential people. Since we seek success, we try to replicate the behavior of successful people.

Core Lessons from the Chapter:

To create better habits, be part of a culture where the behavior you want is the regular behavior and where you have common things with the group already.

Chapter 10: Discovering and Rectifying the Causes of Your Bad Habits

The most important rule to remember to get rid of a bad habit is the inversion of the 2nd Law of Behavior Change. Start by making the bad habit unattractive. Each behavior works on two levels. The first is the superficial craving and the second is the concealed motive, which goes deeper. Our habits serve as contemporary solutions to age-old desires.

The prediction that comes before our habits acts as their cause. This prediction creates a feeling in us that needs to be fulfilled. Predictions work in the following way:

Cue: You notice that the stove is hot.
Prediction: *If I touch it I'll get burned, so I should avoid touching it.*

Cue: You see that the traffic light turned green.
Prediction: *If I step on the gas, I'll make it safely through the intersection and get closer to my destination, so I should step on the gas.*

We need to underline and emphasize the advantages of getting rid of a bad habit to make it appear unattractive.

Habits become attractive to us when we link them with positive feelings and unattractive when we link them with negative feelings. Form a ritual for motivation by engaging in something you enjoy prior to a challenging habit.

Core Lessons from the Chapter:

- Make a bad habit unattractive.

- Emphasize the advantages of getting rid of a bad habit to make it appear unappealing.

- Devise a motivation ritual by engaging in something you like doing right before a challenging habit.

The Third Law: Make It Easy

Chapter 11: Proceed Slowly but Not Backward

The best way to make learning work is by practicing instead of planning. We should give importance to action instead of motion to make progress. We need to take action. Habit formation makes it possible for a behavior to be more automatic through reiteration.

What matters more, is the number of times we have executed a habit than the time span in which we have been doing it. Keep practicing a habit repeatedly until it becomes automatic.

Core Lessons from the Chapter:

- Keep repeating a habit until you start performing it automatically.

Chapter 12: The Law of Least Effort

We need to accomplish more with less effort. The best way to lessen the resistance linked with our habits is to implement environmental design. We can also design our environment in the best possible manner to increase the easiness of actions. The best place to begin a new habit is somewhere that is a part of our daily schedule. It is simpler to build habits when they are part of our life flow. We can easily adopt habits that do not create a lot of friction. For example, we experience higher probability of going to the gym if it is somewhere along our passage to work since it will not create a lot of friction. If it takes even a few more blocks to deviate, then we will have to go out of our way to go the gym and it will become more difficult to go.

When we try to build habits in a high-friction setting, it creates issues. We should try to lessen the friction within our home or office. We cannot focus on a task with a smartphone full of distractions by our side. We may try to do some writing in a busy house. It does not work that way. Human behavior adheres to the Law of Least Effort. We are inclined to select the alternative that necessitates the smallest degree of work.

Design an environment that will facilitate the right thing by making it as easy as possible. Lessen the friction linked with positive behaviors. Less friction will result in easier habits. Boost the friction linked with negative behaviors. High friction will make such habits hard to follow. Optimize your environment so that future actions will be as easy as possible.

To increase friction for bad habits, follow this example. If you watch too much TV, unplug it when you are done. When you feel like watching TV, utter the name of the show you wish to watch loudly. You can leave your phone in the other room while you are working. If it's in the same room, you will keep checking it even when you have no reason to. Prime your environment for the next intended action so that it is ready. Make your bed right after waking up. Clean your toilet before a shower. Clean the dishes right after a meal.

Core Lessons from the Chapter:

- Form an environment where taking the right action is the easiest choice.

- Lessen resistance to good behaviors.

- Increase resistance to bad behaviors.

- Optimize your environment to make future action as easy as possible.

Chapter 13: Use the 2-Minute Rule to Stop Procrastinating

We can complete our habits in a couple of seconds but they will carry on affecting our behavior for minutes or hours later. Several habits happen at decisive moments. Decisive moments are choices that can go two ways. They can lead to either a fruitful or unfruitful day.

The two-minute rule becomes important in this context. It underlines that when we initiate a new habit, it must take less than two minutes to carry it out. When we turn the starting point of a process into a ritual, we can enter the kind of deep concentration that will enable us to achieve greatness. We need to create a habit before trying to improve. A habit needs to exist before it can get better. If we want to build a habit of reading before bed, we can start with the two-minute version i.e., reading just one page. If we want to start yoga, its two-minute version would be to take out our yoga mat. We can start with the two-minute version of any habit and expand from there.

Core Lessons from the Chapter:

- Follow the two-minute rule. Start a new habit by taking less than two minutes to get it going.

- Ritualize the start of a process so that you can slide into the deep concentration needed for great things.

- First create a habit before trying to make it perfect by just starting a small version of it.

Chapter 14: Making Good Habits Irresistible and Bad Ones Impossible

The inversion of the 3rd Law of Behavior Change is making it difficult. A commitment device becomes significant in this context since it refers to a present choice that guarantees improved future behavior. To make future behavior a sure thing, make habits automatic.

Choices that work on a one-time basis, for example, purchasing a new mattress or registering in a savings plan, are sole actions that automate our future habits and lead to amplifying returns over time.

The most efficient and dependable way to ensure the correct behavior is by using technology to automate our behavior.

Core Lessons from the Chapter:

- Make a bad habit difficult.

- Automate your behavior to make future returns possible.

- Use technology to automate your habits.

The 4th Law: Make it Satisfying

Chapter 15: The Fundamental Rule of Behavior Change

The probability of us repeating a behavior is high when the experience is satisfying. The problem with our priorities is that human behavior went through the process of evolution to prefer quick rewards over delayed rewards. The fundamental rule of behavior change is: We repeat what is immediately rewarded. We avoid what is immediately punished.

If we want a habit to stay, we need to feel successful even if it is in a tiny manner. The initial three laws of behavior change (i.e., make it obvious, attractive, and easy) boost the chances of a behavior being carried out. The 4th Law, make it satisfying, boosts the chances of a behavior being reiterated next time.

Core Lessons from the Chapter:

- To make a habit last, try to feel successful right after it.

Chapter 16: Continuing Good Habits Daily

Making progress can lead to a lot of satisfaction. Visual measures, which might include shifting paper clips, hairpins, or marbles from one jar/container to another when you are done with a small task (one item per task) can be extremely satisfying since it offers obvious evidence of one's progress.

The Power of Habit Trackers

Habit tracking is measuring whether we performed a habit or not. The simplest way to do it is to use a calendar and mark every day that we adhere to our routine.

Advantages of Habit Tracking

The first advantage is that it is obvious and tracking our last action can give rise to an activator for the next one. When you see the tracker or the visual cues, it will act as a reminder to take that action again. Habit tracking also enables us to be honest.

Habit tracking is attractive. When we notice that we are progressing, we feel motivated to keep going that way.

The third advantage is that it is satisfying. The very act of tracking a habit and crossing off an item after performing it is extremely satisfying.

The How

Habit tracking is not everyone's cup of tea. It can feel like a burden to adopt a new habit and track it as well. In this technological age, a lot of tracking is automatic such as our credit card statements and different apps. We should manually track only the most significant of our habits. The best way to measure a habit is right after it has been carried out.

The formula for habit stacking + habit tracking:

After [CURRENT HABIT], I will [TRACK MY HABIT].

Examples:

After I make a sales call, I will shift one paper clip from one container to another.

After finishing one type of exercise in the gym, I will write it down in my workout journal.

After I wash my plate, I will note what I had.

Keep it Going

Try to avoid breaking a habit. Keep it going. Don't miss twice in a row. If you miss once, try to go back as early as possible. The ability to measure something does not make it the most significant thing. Only measure your most significant habits manually.

Core Lessons from the Chapter:

- Track your habits by measuring them.

- You can do it by marking an X on a calendar on the days you did it.

- Avoid missing twice. If you miss once, get back on track immediately.

- Only measure the most significant habits.

<u>The formula for habit stacking + habit tracking:</u>

After [CURRENT HABIT], I will [TRACK MY HABIT].

Chapter 17: The Importance of Having an Accountability Partner

The inversion of the 4th Law of Behavior Change is to make it unsatisfying. The probability of repeating a bad habit is less if it is unsatisfying or painful. An accountability partner can help us experience a quick cost of a lack of action. Others' opinions of us are extremely significant. We do not want them to have an unfavorable opinion of us.

You can use a habit contract to include a social cost of any behavior. If you breach the habit contract, it will be humiliating since your behavior will be painful and public. When we know that another person is monitoring us, it can act like a strong motivator.

Core Lessons from the Chapter:

- Make bad habits unsatisfying.

- Have an accountability partner who can reprimand you if you take a step in the wrong direction.

- We can activate a social cost to a behavior by using a habit contract.

High Level Strategies: How to Be Great, Not Just Good

Chapter 18: Talent and the Extent of Genes' Roles

We need to select the correct field of competition to increase our chances for success. Everything is not for everyone. Going forward is easy if you choose the correct habit. Everything will become a challenge if you choose the wrong habit. We cannot change genes. They offer a strong advantage in positive conditions and a severe disadvantage in negative conditions.

When our habits synchronize with our natural abilities, they are easier. Select the habits that truly suit you. Play to your strengths. Choose a game that capitalizes on your strengths. If you cannot identify a game that gives you an advantage, devise one. Genes do not take away the requirement for hard work. They unveil it by telling us what we should work hard on.

Core Lessons from the Chapter:

- Choose the right field of competition to be successful.

- Choose the right habit.

- Select the habits that suit you.

- Work hard.

Chapter 19: The Goldilocks Rule: How to Keep the Motivation Alive in Life and Work

The Goldilocks rule underlines that humans go through the highest degree of motivation while dealing with tasks that are at the brim of their present abilities. We need to note that the biggest challenge to success is boredom rather than failure. When habits become part of our schedule, we lose interest in them and do not derive satisfaction from them. We experience boredom.

All of us can work hard amidst motivation. What really matters is the resolve to continue when work does not excite us anymore. Professionals adhere to their routine. Amateurs get distracted by life.

Core Lessons from the Chapter:

- Keep working even when work is not exciting anymore.

- Adhere to your schedule.

Chapter 20: Negative Aspects of Forming Good Habits

Mastery = Habits + Intentional Practice

The advantage of habits is that we can get things done without even thinking. The disadvantage is that we might start ignoring small mistakes. We can stay aware of our performance over time by using reflection and review.

When we adhere closely to an identity, it becomes increasingly difficult to surpass it.

Core Lessons from the Chapter:

- Use reflection and review to keep your performance consistent.

Conclusion

An atomic habit can change our life. When we start small, we can build the foundation of truly remarkable change. We can grow from one atomic habit by letting them multiply. It can give rise to a chain which keeps growing longer and improving our lives. Truly great change will start at some point. If we want to change our life, we should start today. Nothing is impossible for us if we learn and try to discipline ourselves. No one can accomplish anything by dreaming only. We have to support our dreams by making proper plans and focusing on the tiny details. The strategies in this book teach us how to do that effectively.

Made in the USA
Middletown, DE
25 November 2019